THE JOURNEY TO *LE REPENTIR*:

POEMS IN FOUR NARRATIVE SEQUENCES

# THE JOURNEY TO *LE REPENTIR*:

# POEMS IN FOUR NARRATIVE SEQUENCES

## MARK McWATT

PEEPAL TREE

First published in Great Britain in 2009
Peepal Tree Press Ltd
17 King's Avenue
Leeds LS6 1QS
UK

ISBN 13: 9781845230814

Supported by
ARTS COUNCIL
ENGLAND

# CONTENTS

Four things were created by God simultaneously, to wit:
the Universe, the Angelic Nature, Time and the Empyrean
Heavens...

> — Saint Thomas Aquinas

... we pronounce joy like a word of our own.

> — Wallace Stevens

Every inclination to crawl or creep
upon immensity is nameless. Yet it is sometimes called Birth,
it is sometimes called Death.

> — Wilson Harris

# INTRODUCTION

This is a collection of poems written in the years since the publication of *The Language of Eldorado* in 1994. Around the year 2000 I realized that I was working towards at least two different goals: the first of these was that the book would be in four parts, with each part containing a central narrative poem or sequence of poems and this would be balanced or counterpoised or embellished with other poems. The other goal that began to be clear was that the collection would have an autobiographical dimension. I knew that I had to be careful here because I have long been aware that, while it is true that most of the poems I write have an autobiographical significance, at the same time my poetry has always resisted the purely autobiographical (i.e.: that which is absolutely true), so that it is impossible to identify very closely what I write with the events of my life. What tend to emerge are glimpses of a fictional life which nevertheless correspond with – or suggest in some way – aspects of my own experience. Thus, for instance, the four sections of the book correspond roughly with four phases of my life so far: 1) childhood, 2) adolescence and early adulthood, 3) maturity and finally 4) the approach of old age.

There are several themes woven into the four sections and also into the several other movements going on at the same time, for example from rainy season to dry season; from sexual innocence to (sometimes transgressive) sexual experience; from outdoors to indoors; from the natural world to the world inside the head, etc. I am hoping that all of this manages to suggest the complexity and variety of lived experience and of any art that reflects it.

The first section is called "Mercator" and the poems alternate in perspective between that of a nameless Elizabethan sea captain and adventurer (based in part on my readings of Walter Raleigh's adventures in Guiana) who finds himself seeking Eldorado in the rivers of Guyana's north-west district and, on the other hand, the semi-autobiographical subject, a boy living and going to school and discovering self and world in the same north-west district.

The second section, called "The Dark Constellation", deals in more lyrical manner with the discoveries of love and learning and awakening sexuality in the context of Guyana's landscape, especially the rivers, the map of which has been permanently engraved in my mind since childhood. The power and joy associated with these elements are sometimes confusingly undercut (now as then) by dark hints of failure and disappointment associated, perhaps, with flaws and deviations in the perception of self and world. This duality, initiated here, persists throughout the book.

Section three, "The Museum of Love", centres around a maturing awareness of time and the way it controls everything. This section is about maturity on the personal as well as the national level and there is a sequence of poems on "Independence". The central narrative here is set inside a museum and focuses on the inevitable changes and losses that are the results of time and the (often futile) strategies we adopt to circumvent them. However much we revolt against the pain inflicted by time we are always found, in the end, to have conspired with time to create our own disappointments and frustrations.

The narrative sequence at the heart of the final section of the book, "*Le Repentir*", concerns the story of Pierre Louis De Saffon (1724 – 1784), a Frenchman who accidentally killed his brother in a duel and ended up in exile in Demerara. He eventually purchased two sugar plantations which he named *La Penitence* and *Le Repentir* to signify his guilt and penance for his sin of fratricide. Part of *Le Repentir* plantation became (appropriately?) the main cemetery of the city of Georgetown. There is also a personal connection for me in that my paternal grandmother benefited from the terms of De Saffon's will: he directed that his fortune be used to educate some of the orphan or semi-orphan daughters of indigent white families in the colony. She apparently qualified. The other poems in the section explore the ideas of mid-life crisis and attendant sexual anxieties and thoughts about old-age, guilt and death.

Mark McWatt

2008 – 05 – 30

# PART I

# MERCATOR

# UNIVERSE

This is my song of the universe, of the past
that is now and the future that is never, but
mostly about a place and a mind inter-
penetrated through a membrane of wonder,
a dark fistula of dream through which flows,
back and forth, a boy and the palpable matter
of his first and widest world... Think of a garden
invaded by a black creek, its flowering orchids,
grown in coconut husks, floated off the trunk
of the grapefruit tree and trundled down to the river,
to bob among the palm seeds and the driftwood
and the anxious ripples of the tacouba, half-
submerged in the eye of the frantic bow-man,
dancing with his big paddle and signalling
the steersman to keep hard right. And that night,
in the flooded garden at the tide of the full moon,
the blue bunderie crabs march like a helpless army
into quakes and baskets, into steaming pots,
into the widening eyes of children, as sleepless
as Christmas eve. It is the North West district
of Guyana (before there was "Region One");
it was the 1950s (before 'massa day' done).
It was that hill of red earth, those misty mornings
of wet grass and Wellington boots, those rivers,
creeks, stellings, that dark Rubber Walk... that
wrapped themselves around my hopeless heart
and, to this day, have not let go...

                              So the first part
of my poem's life tells of that universe, of memories
of its magic, in the compound at Mabaruma, in
the schoolhouse, where teacher Stephanie's chalk

drawings on blackboards never to be erased
helped define for me the life of books, of competitive
learning, of the sensuous adventure of knowledge
that has never let me go;  the only school before
university where I sat in the same classroom with girls
and loved them, and longed for them and got my mouth
washed out with soap because the nuns told my parents
the unspeakable things I said I would like to do
with Cecilia Joseph, with Olinda Santiago...

But I always knew that world did not begin
with me: I was told that red hill contained bones
older than our dreams, and later, when I had read
my universe into a different context and could see
its links to other worlds, I dreamt for it my own
moment of genesis, when a vessel from another
adventure sailed into the Barima in rainy season...

# MERCATOR

*(For George Lamming)*

## I

A single vessel wrapped in a cloud of mist
stood on the coldly boiling quicksilver
of another unknown river lashed by rain.
Its master on the quarterdeck looked up
and imagined that the invisible mast-tops
had pierced a calm blue heaven above the rain;
to get there was simply a matter of ascent,
foot above foot and hand above clasping hand,
each movement finite, achievable –
yet the journey itself as impossible as hope...
The master was familiar with "impossible":
perhaps "impossible" is the end of all
adventures, whether the fancied quest
be for gold, or human love, or heaven.
"Impossible", the master thought, is the signature
of human flesh in these rain-sotted rivers
he had thought to claim and capture
– for what? For a monarch safe in bed
far beyond the sunrise? For a people ready
to swarm like vermin over edible landscapes?
For that chimera "glory", itself closer to nothing
than these rain-fashioned bubbles on the river
below him that endure for less time than
a single breath? For Countrye? For the advance
of knowledge? No, knowledge is just another
beckoning harlot ready to ripen flesh and soul
with sin and disease, and pluck them for the grave...

For nothing, then: for the mere digestion
of days, the eating and the defecation of time
to give the illusion of growth, of achievement.

The master strained through the mists
to see the banks of the river they would
one day call "Barima", a minor serpent
in that wriggling nest of streams that empties
into this wide bight of continental coast,
and whose lore and venom had entered
all their hearts and sang the sweet song
of golden venture in their very blood. And
here he was: the river seethed like liquid silver,
the banks, when the rain permitted sight of them,
were an endless sea of idiot green.
Elsewhere were light and shade, but in his soul
deep darkness – far heavier than gold...

The morrow morn brought the long-famished sunlight
that pierced, devoured the lingering shapes of mist;
the master, in a damp and musty tunic
dredged from the bottom of his trunk,
stood in the sunshine and surveyed the scene:
on the port side the mangroves stretched
flat and endless, suggesting a vast swamp,
the mighty cesspool of a scowering continent;
to starboard the land appeared to rise
behind the swamp. Hills, the possibility
of brown or red or yellow earth and stones,
perhaps, that glint in sunlight; fresh game
might wander there, and sweet, clear water...
Strange how one's focus always narrows
to such pitiful pleasures as food and drink, the smell
of wood-smoke and of fresh-turned soil.

# HELLO MARABUNTA
## (*For My Mother*)

In our first house in Mabaruma
there were no ceilings, and the walls
stopped far short of the roof so all the rooms
could breathe the same current of air...
I loved to climb to the magical space
we boys had found on top of our built-in
wardrobe: we named it "Hello Marabunta"
(having encountered a nest of those wasps
the first time up there). We would climb
up there to hide, to sulk, to read
forbidden comic books, or just to feel alone,
unreachable. That narrow space overlooked
our room, our parents' room, the windowless
storeroom and pantry from which arose
the smell of ripening fruit, and that passage-
space that had become a dining room...
I loved to be up there alone, when my brothers
roamed the compound in quest of adventure,
or had already drifted off to sleep.

One night, when my father was gone
on one of his week-long trips up-river
and the lights were long turned off,
I climbed up silently to Hello Marabunta,
taking my pillow with me, and stretched out
on the unpainted, dusty planks and became
master of all the magic spaces of that house
until, settling down on my pillow
to dream of all my life's perfections,
I heard a quiet sobbing that could only be
my mother: I crept to the corner
that overlooked their room, but looking down,
all I could see in the darkness was the top

of the mosquito net, though the sobbing
was clearer, soft and sad, and suddenly
my world became far less than perfect.
I listened as she wept, all alone in that big bed;
I could think of no reason for her pain.
My brothers in their sweet oblivion slept
and I had to listen, until it started to rain
– rain  drumming on the iron roof swept away
all other sounds. I knew I could never ask her
why she wept, but I felt her sadness
become a part of me…

When, in the half-light of dawn
I woke to hear her stirring, I quickly climbed
down to my bed. I think I knew instinctively,
alone, up there on Hello Marabunta,
what I have since confirmed: that it is not
always possible to name the hurt
that makes us weep, sometimes it's best to sob
quietly, uncomforted and, just as the rain
took away the sound of my mother weeping,
to join the many causes of our pain
to the one unending sorrow of the world.

The master stood on the red earth
of a hill the natives called "Mabaruma",
so distant from his land of birth; a large flat rock
overhung by large and leaning boulders
from which leafy vines and tendrils dangled,
reminded him of his passion as a young man
for the stage — another engine of the restless
imagination: he remembered the feigned struggles
of masters Kyd and Marlowe — action and sound effects,
blood and colours and the seduction of poetry
squandered on the illiterate groundlings,
drunk with framed pictures of lives and passions
that touched them, but that they could never touch.
It was like a hundred new worlds
roosting in the rafters of their own city, to be
gaped at for ha'pennies in the squalid safety
of home. He remembered painted east
and west and Will Shakespeare's Denmark, Rome.
What plays will men write about the world
where he now stands? What can one write
about endless, boring rain, a few squat savages,
red earth like blood upon their calloused hands?
How could their loves and murders matter
to the hedges and hierarchies of home?

Ah, but the manufactured beauty
of the London stage had helped to lesson
the eye that measured now and judged
this other world across the ocean sea.
These bare-bosomed girls would shock
the finer senses of English men like him
and summon wild imaginings of venereal

pleasures at the tip of that inverted fork
of sunburnt flesh that straddles this red earth.
But such images betray the mind that makes them:
they seem more like trees than humans –
soulless wood rather than sentient flesh –
they never could displace the radiance
of Tamburlaine, nor cause the mind to mis-
remember the soft despair of young Ophelia:
her gentleness, her long, light, lovely hair...

## KANAIMA / TIGER
### (*For Richard and David*)

In the darkest middle of the rubber walk
where the interweave of overhanging branches
was thick above the road, the four schoolboys
walking home (loitering in the roadside bush,
collecting shiny rubber seeds in their wooden pods)
suddenly stopped – movement, talk, breath,
all stopped: for there in the road, yards ahead,
stood a black tiger. He had appeared out of nowhere.
When I first saw him he was simply there; his cold
green eyes looked straight at us, four human statues
with shoulder-slung bookbags and gaping mouths.
He looked long, then turned his head and strode
into the bush on the other side of the road.

It was the first time any of us had seen
a black tiger. For the next two weeks they sent
the Land Rover to collect us after school,
making of the magical rubber walk
a ninety-second blur of dark green gloom
incensed with the damp smell of leaves. But
we were soon walking again, collecting rubber
seeds and daring each other to step
into the undergrowth and enter the darker
realm of the tiger. "It wasn't a tiger,"
Jude Santiago had said, the day after we saw it;
"remember how he watch at we and think?
My father say tigers don't think. Was
Kanaima. Kanaima was looking for somebody:
lucky it wasn't we." And he was right,
the creature did look at us and think.
So it was Kanaima... And yet something

in my head made Jude's dark certainty
impossible for me. My father was certain
it wasn't Kanaima; Jude was certain that it was,
and mine was that painful uncertainty
that helped define my childhood plight:
Caught between their "wrong" and our "right".

Now time and distance have tamed the memory,
and the fear has drained away: I have
long since learned to say "jaguar" instead of
"tiger" (in contexts where that kind of accuracy
matters). But whenever I rummage in the deepest
drawer of childhood memories, I still
cannot decide whether it was tiger or Kanaima
that looked hard at us that day, that
found us wanting and calmly walked away.

("*Kanaima*" in Amerindian lore, is an avenging spirit that can assume any form
it wants as it moves through the forest in pursuit of its human victims.)

# MERCATOR III

Like their women, the master thought,
this land is for force: there is no place
for scruple's gentle touch nor the moral trap
of care. Take what you want, and where –
rip the red earth for gold, the trees
for timber, tear the women's sullied flesh
for pleasure. This is a place, but not
a countrye; there is no throned power to curb
nor oppose my will. This forest requires
no licence to hunt its deer. These "things"
tricked out in human shapes have yet no idea
of "human", no faith, no sacred self to violate
the violator. All that matters here is matter:
what hand can touch, what fist can seize
or smash; what axe and pick can hew or mine.
It is all equally for our consumption, like the
daily ration of spirits to numb the horror
of the loss of home. It's the only way
to undermine the hubris of compassion.

Even the rivers here are too natural,
wild and undisciplined – this meanders
like a drunken scullion pissing down an alley,
splashing itself all over the landscape,
innocent of the need for human engineering
to restrain its boisterousness with dam and levee;
it should be pulled tight like a halyard through
a straight canal or two of uniform and navigable depth,
its ragged seaward end back-spliced with harbour walls
to give it shape and definition, and purpose, most of all.
The things of nature, the master thought, should
be made manageable, like nature in his own far land:

where rivers do not change their channel with each tide,
and forested isles do not float on two fathoms
of water to beguile the senses and confuse the brain;
where is no drunken prodigality of rain...
This may well be the first real vessel this river
has ever seen, and it should show more respect:
it is the God-given authority of a mighty queen
that sent and keeps it here – not mindless nature,
sprawled like a harlot, beckoning and infecting all,
confounding all attempt at lawful measurement...

## ANATOMICAL

*(For Nickie Calistro)*

Each mid-morning at Mabaruma school
classes were interrupted and we joined a queue
behind the building, waiting to receive
a large mug of thick, frothy milk, mysteriously
brewed from powder, and two sweet biscuits
fished from a huge, shiny tin. I'd overheard
Sister once explaining to my mother
that she let us line up with the others
"so they wouldn't feel left out" – and I
was happy, not just because of my hunger
to be like everyone else, but I loved
the milk, the biscuits and the break from class…

And it was in that queue one morning
that Nickie Valenzuela (the squat, round-faced
boy behind me in the line) turned to
Rita Stoll and asked, loud enough
for many of us to hear: "You like
how I play with your pussy last night?"
Those near us in the line laughed knowingly
but I, not yet ten and having only brothers,
had never entered the labyrinth of those words
and laughed much louder than the others
– and was still laughing when I held out
my mug to be filled. One of the two
big girls serving (with Sister looking on
between them) said: "And what's so funny, Mark?"
And me, savouring their smiling curiosity:
"Oh, nothing – just that Rita liked
when Nickie played with her pussy last night…"
Silence and consternation all around

29

And me in shock at the sudden transformation
of the mood...

          They always say that school
is for learning — and I learnt a lot that day,
beginning with Nickie's harshly whispered "Fool!" —
the girls covering their mouths in giggling wonder
and Sister sternly making the sign of the cross...
Well, never one to mourn the loss of innocence,
I consider that the punishments received — the
lashes at school, the suspension for two days,
my mother washing out my mouth with soap —
were worth it in the end, as passport
to that sensuous world of anatomical  wonder
where Nickie and I, recovered from our shame,
would sit with a few of the older boys under
the schoolyard tree and give a common name
to each fleshly urge — more of the blanks filled in —
and all this long before the grown-ups had their say
and cursed it all and turned it into sin...

## MERCATOR IV

"Buried Midshipman Banks today", the Master
wrote in his journal. "He was ill with a tertian fever
before we left the Gulf of Paria and worsened
after a week on this river of rain that breeds
damp mists and foul miasmas: contagions
sufficient to soften and infect the brain. The last
few days he could keep nothing down, and his skin
shrank and tightened about awkward, shocking bones
– we buried little more than bones, wrapped
and tied like a parcel. Covering them with wet,
red earth, his fellows piled a heap of heavy stones
round the base of a wooden cross that bears his name.
We said the prayers. God grant that his freed soul
has already fled from here – in which case who
among us would not wish to take his place…?
Instead of digging precious metals, we deposit
in this earth our own dead remains… Poor wretch:
so far from home, so close to Eldorado, and now
so mercifully freed from mortal pains…"
The men in the pinnace returned today,
having reached a fierce cataract that could not
be ascended, where they also lost the boy
to a band of savage warriors who attacked
when they were seeking a portage. Until
that disaster, nothing! More swampy banks
and red-earth hills and groups of squalid savages
tricked out in ornaments of seeds and shell
and feather – but not gold. No sign of any city
nor hill of shining crystall on these banks; some
other river, perhaps; the men are anxious
to leave this one at once. They say it is a place
of gloom and damp and death, and grumble:

"What if there be no Eldorado?" What indeed?
What if Raleigh and the Spaniards spun these tales
to save their skins — or reputations — or else
to promote the enterprise of this new world,
which each succeeding expedition, seeking gold,
will help to hew into more human shape, until
great cities straddle rivers such as this, and
trading vessels crowd their well-dredged ports.
And somewhere on their banks — as there,
perhaps — a theatre thrusts its hollow wooden tube
into the air, as tall as that great tree... And English
players, imported for the season, tramp up
and down its stage declaiming Master Shakespeare...
Perhaps we were born too soon, before
all this is conceived; t'were better to be here
when it's accomplished — and yet, these very thoughts,
perhaps, be sufficient conception of that dream
of English cities far from England's shore...
I swear, if ever Christian settlement should sprout
its roofs and towers on this dark river, it will be
in fulfilment of my dreaming now and here:
perhaps that's what the adventure's all about...

# KORIABO

Once in rainy season
when sky and river are one,
I pause and smell your rank breath
borne on the wet breeze,
and I shiver at the whisper it conveyed
of your age and life and longing.
You whose vast memory
I enter, perhaps as a recent, ephemeral blur,
the touch of boat or body
hardly registering, as I watch the wind
blow across your wet back
causing goosebumps of exploding raindrops,
and I think it is such a love
— and expressed like that —
that I long for.

I exhale audibly
(a gesture lost in the love-song of the rain)
and resume paddling.
I'm comforted by the perception
that, like you and the wind
and the rain, I have somewhere
to go. And who can say
that the love that I find
at the inscrutable end of my journey
will not be as shiveringly perfect
as that cold kiss of the wind
on your bare, brown back?

Or is it all delirium? The fever
of a dead midshipman humming in my brain?
When the forested hillside next opens its red mouth,
will it be to consume my fleshless bones?
And why not, as that would be no steep loss
to anyone in England. No grieving wife
nor desolate mistress do I leave to mourn.
None such have I ever caused to stand a whole tide
on a windy, shingled shore to watch the ship
with her departing love, slide beneath that line
'twixt sea and sky. The only she I ever loved died
long before I found the words in me that might
have persuaded her to become my bride.
Now I have all the words and more, but none
to woo with them; it is as well, for with her
died all my love of living women. It is less pain
and safer for me now to love instead those feigned
queens and princesses that tread the wooden
stage and speak unforgettable poetry. There's
symmetry in the fact that I now pace this deck,
another wooden stage, my mind filled with poetry
so strange in the vast indifference of this land.
Call her Ophelia, the image of my desire:
for her alone I make my quest, I blow the fire
of longing in every sailor's eye: "The gold,
The gold! It's the thing we come to find…"
But if the truth be told, I care nothing for riches,
nor for fame: were the queen's own sword
on my shoulder now and she bidding me to rise
in some gilded abbey, the glory of that moment
would not fill my hungry heart so much
as to hear Ophelia say again, "My Lord, I have

remembrances of yours that I have long'd long
to redeliver..." And I fancy I can save her soft
white soul before the water rinse it out her eyes...

# ARUKA

All the rain long
the world wept
like a wide wound in the soft
of you; I kept closer than skin
to the warmth of your wetness
and drew in the rippling wake of me
that bateau loud with the laughter
of blunt boys and melting girls
on the point of collapsing with the merry
of the raining time
when, river, you whipped around,
heavy with tacoubas and the green garnish of
water hyacinths, and confronted us all
with the sudden terror of love.

And look how the when folded
then, like a bateau foundered in rippling wake,
the whole crisp moment slipped like new currency
into the pocket of always,
of never… It is always so with the love of rivers.
It is always so sudden, like
drowning or like the drift
of snake venom in the warm dilations
of a hopeless heart. The desire
to die for you is not gesture
nor pose, but the pure minted truth
of our nature – true to every vein
and every reach of river
into the heart of other,
into the funnel
of the trumpet of time.

And if you were not Aruka
of my childhood delight
but just a wild memory of rain,
it would not be the same;
yet it would be *exactly*
the same.

# MERCATOR VI

Close-hauled near the mouth of the river,
the vessel making sluggish way in a light
ocean breeze, the master in his cabin
breathes deeply and checks his charts. The next
river to the east is called Guiana: "It looks",
the master thinks, "a longer and a wider stream,
perhaps it will plumb deeper the unknown
interior places of this amphibious land;
to where the soggy coastal plain gives way
to hills, where farms, with their crops and hedges
roll right down to the river's sunlit edges;
where may dwell folk who have seen Manoa's
golden towers and may be persuaded to point
the direction and say how long the march be
to its fabled gate. Oh, the dream of conquest,
almost vanquished by disappointment and by rain,
finds life anew and warms my blood again:
Orrinocco, Guiana, Dessikepe and the next
and all the lesser waters in between, I would
that many more such as these were shown
on the chart of this savage coast: penetrate
them all would I, and reap more pleasure
from the rape of rivers, from thrusting hard
into virgin realms than from all England's women
severally laid flat and subject to my will.
To the wide Guiana river then, and
may the tide that takes us 'cross her bar
be the flood-tide of such a change of fortune
that the world will never be the same hereafter..."

# DROWNED LOVES

1

She was a schoolgirl, thirteen years of age,
Olinda Santiago; her younger brother, Jude,
was in my class. I watched her sometimes
in the shop, or when she would pass the school-
yard carrying a covered basket, her broad, bare
feet wonderful on the hot hard road. I told
my ten-year-old self I was in love with her –
and now she was dead; she fell into the river
at Barima landing and disappeared – until
the next low tide revealed her flotsam form
sprawled on the mud between the piles. We all
went down to see her – skin stretched tight,
her budding breasts exposed, her face veiled
by the tangle of her long hair. It was my first
drowning, my first shocking encounter with
this version of the thief called death, and
I wept at the stillness he had wrought upon a form
so full before with the restless itch of life, who bore,
so excitingly past our schoolyard, all my dreams
of love. Jude, who never said much anyway,
now stood silent as an iron bollard next to me.
We watched some men, knee-deep in river mud,
retrieve the sorry bundle of wasted years...
our childish faces long and wet with tears.

2

When we got to the village up the creek
the savages were gathered on a ledge of rock
beside the water: a young girl had drowned
and her naked form lay lifeless on the stone.
She had the beauty of youth and long, black hair,
and these alone spoke unbidden words into my ear:
"Soft you now, the fair Ophelia"; and all the freight
of feeling loaded in the vessel of that play
discharged upon me, and I turned my face away,
softly cursing Shakespeare for this unwanted access
of sympathy that could not but impair my mission,
my resolve to steer into the wild heart of this
continent, and reap by force whatever riches
I would find guarded and protected there...
On that rock, up a black and unnamed creek
I knew I was no conqueror of men. I decided
then that the quest at last was over: even if
we spent another year wandering in these waters,
there would be no sacking of Manoa, no looting
of Eldorado gold. Instead, and everywhere,
there would be savages looking and feeling more
and more like me. This drowned Ophelia of the creek
has taught my too-soft heart a fatal compassion.
It was time to go: the crew's resolve was weak,
and rape and conquest suddenly out of fashion.

# EXILE

It was like being summoned suddenly
from idle, barefoot play
to put on "good" clothes to meet some
important visitor from town... that day
when they told me they were sending me away –
from them, from home, from here, from
this my universe – to live in the city where
I must go to school and try to get
a scholarship to go to another school...
But I was already lost, just thinking about it,
and something umbilical that anchored me
to that place – and to all that was carefree –
snapped, and I said stiff, awkward farewells
to people, places, things that I seemed to be seeing
for the first time. I was told not
to cry, that uncles and grandparents would
love me and look after me and...

So began my everlasting exile
when I stepped onto that fortnightly steamer
and sailed out of the Mora passage, out
of the Waini estuary, along the coast to town...
Oh I saw everyone and everything again,
at the  holidays... was eventually joined
by my brothers as they reached the age;
then they built a house and the whole family
lived in town... But before I knew the word
I knew I would always be an exile – holding
back tears, repeating a fierce vow
that if anyone was going to be hurt, it

would be me, only me… because I can take it…
and fifty years later, I still sometimes repeat
that vow and remember that first voyage
into the eternal exile of my heart.

# MERCATOR

## *Homecoming*

By the time the master coaxed his vessel
into the broad estuary of the Thames, he was
numb from a surfeit of contrary emotions:
the disappointment of a failed expedition,
the bitter relief at the approach of home
(bitter in part because of the freezing fog
that clung to their limbs and damp clothing),
the thought of what he must say to those
whose golden hopes had sponsored the adventure…
the thought of the few paltry proofs of his
having been anywhere – let alone at the gates
of Manoa… True there were trinkets aplenty,
a few forest creatures in miserable cages,
a few shivering savages stink in their own
shit and vomit, huddled in a hold somewhere
– mere remnants: there had been eight of them,
now there were five; two had died and one,
a merc boy, had killed himself, having been
horribly abused by two of his men, drunk
on spirits and desire and unable to wait
a few weeks for the flesh of England to sate
their lust. He would have had them killed
there and then, but for what? The victim
was only a savage, of one being with trees
and snakes and baboons and waterfalls
– no loyal subject of any king or potentate,
no child of Christ. In the end the two culprits
felt only the lash of the master's tongue
which bruised neither flesh nor spirit
but rather bred a surly contempt, which altered
for the worse both them and their chastiser…

And now, with the world wrapped in a cold mist,
they approached again the brutal truth of home.
The first thing they learned, even before
the sails were lowered, was that the queen
had died some several weeks before and
there was a king called James on England's throne.
For the master this seemed a final betrayal.
He realized that it had been the image of his queen
that had sustained and guided his weakening spirit
in those rotting rivers and rain-soaked forests;
it was a picture of her lovely form in his mind
that smiled indulgently at his feeble endeavours,
and now she was gone; his thoughts returned
at once to that savage girl drowned in a black creek,
her naked, lifeless form forlorn on a hard outcrop
of grey stone: how his mind had contrasted that scene
with the living wonder of his queen... and now,
to surmise that by that time the sweet mistress
of his will may already have been dead...
The master looked around once before stepping,
for the last time, off his ship; the thing
most certain in his mind was that never
would he sail again upon the ocean sea; the one
event to which his life looked forward now was death,
that which would make him equal at the end
with the monarch his heart and soul had sought to serve.
With a wild look on his yet sunburnt face
and a muttered curse that made him seem a madman,
he stepped grimly onto the wooden dock of home.

# GRUMMAN GOOSE

I liked to watch the white spray
like the wild wake of a speedboat
racing up the river — until spray disappeared
and the squat silver hull slowly lifted
above the water, above the trees on the bank,

above my capacity to imagine the experience
from inside, as it glinted in the sunlight,
banking against the blue emptiness of sky...

The weekly Grumman Goose taking off
on the Barima fuelled the hopeless dreams
of a schoolboy, head in the clouds, longing
for the adventure of such speed and flight
and the magical abandonment of earth.

The dream came true unexpectedly,
one day at the end of an idle August:
"Pack, you're going to town on tomorrow's plane."
Incredulous, unable to respond, I fly
upstairs to my bedroom, jump into bed
and daydream of heaven — "Are you packing?"
— back to earth and time and the tedium
of intervening hours...
Finally next day, which seemed like years later,
the pilot looks at me, hefts me aboard: "I'd say
seventy pounds", and the co-pilot scribbles
on a pad... We cast off from the stelling,
gather speed, the windows blinded with spray...
Then a different sound and movement
as I watch the trees fall away and see
my universe the way I imagined God did:

rivers retreating into dark ribbons, fancifully
curled and twisted, the forest like
a huge dish of steamed broccoli, cooling
in the breeze… and up into the clouds,
the bright blue, the wonder…

Somehow I sensed in my heart the importance
of separation, the advantage of height and dis-
tance, the wonderful cleavage between self and world.
Perhaps it was only an illusion, but never again
would the imperatives of earth seem oppressive,
nor its obstacles insuperable… The eighteen-
hour steamer trip was shrunk to just one hour,
and when the Grumman landed on the Demerara,
wound down the wheels and ascended the ramp,
I had already readjusted to the loneliness of town
and I smiled at my new discovery:

If big rivers could become as tear-tracks
down a green face – then tears themselves,
and the hurt that prompted them, could easily
be nothing… a dream. I knew then
I would always seek comfort in solitude
and distance. Who, after all, needed human love
in that intense, pure light, in the vastness
of sky over the rivers and forests of home?

II

THE DARK CONSTELLATION

# ANGELIC

For me there was never any final choosing
among angels. I loved them all.
The long-haired ones who did not look
like me filled my heart with desire
long before I knew what love meant;
and those that could have been mirrors
— all knees and flashing fingers and bravado —
I felt I could die for. These were all
angels of distance, though, because I learnt
never to get too close, never to touch —
as if one could be burnt by angels…
Wrapped in my cocoon of chaste longing,
I learnt to decline angels – like
Latin nouns – exhilarated in a felt
mastery – so that when I dreamt of angels
it was to re-enter the ancient question:
how many could dance on the head of a pin?
Or in and out of the valves of my heart?

But there came a time
when half of my angels had to become
a secret, hidden in the cold cupboard
of feigned indifference,
waiting for now – or for never.

# THE DARK CONSTELLATION

Came a time
in restless mid-adolescence
when I began to discern – or imagine –
the possibility of difference,
of letting go that dream of hands
that held, helped, sculpted, defined
the self that I could never see...

Like a buzzing kite in a sudden
wind-lull, I heard my sweet song of self
falter, as when the loud treble
of my childhood voice broke
and drifted into pockets of embarrassed
silence... I was a sigh
uttered into the calm twilight of an evening,
dreading, yet welcoming an inner darkness.

Who knows, at that age,
where ideas and images come from?
I imagined a dark constellation
somewhere in the approaching night
– inscrutable suns and planets – that influenced
my life and longing, that made
me mark forever time
and season and mood and that contrary
motion that would help define me,
swimming against the tide...

And in the dark trough of night
came the doubt
came the mystery of hurt without
physical wounds, came the laughter

of others, the feeding on rich dreams,
as the wing-touch of the vampire bat,
just below the radar of sleeping senses,
fed on the flow of blood;
came the dancing in dark hallways
came the hammock of soft snoring
came the questions and suggestions
and the lore of night-fishermen
and hospital porters and desperate women
who walk the drunken pavements...

And memories – or perhaps dreams –
of all those others in tents,
in sleeping school-rooms, in
idle boats on the morning river:
"He's my brother" one said to me,
proud, as we watched the perfect dive
from the bridge of the steamer into the Aruka river.
These things came to all of us
but only I consumed them
like a teenager on a binge,
seeking the strength to resist
the mighty efforts of love...

And the dark constellation
kept my heart pure
amidst all the waste of youth;
amidst the sickness,
in the shit and the vomit
and the nights of fever...
So that when it was time to face it all
and undo the harm, and shuck
the embarrassing underwear of false pride
and pacify the weepers

and prepare the holocaust of hope
I lent the strength of my arm,
the spirit of sacrifice,
the wanton bravado of hopeless longing...

And it is only now,
on the cusp of a new age
when I can sense a destination of sorts
around the next bend,
that I can summon it all
into the calm acknowledgement of self.
Sometimes I feel I should ask
forgiveness: but I know that in truth
there is nothing to forgive...

# BELOVED OF THE RIVERS
## (*A Fictional Encounter in Ten Poems*)

1

You sat on a tree
that hung over the river
fishing for me.

I took the hook
and I hauled you in-
to the net of my book.

Fallen into fiction
you're now trapped with me
in this self-contradiction.

And there's nothing I can do
within rock and swift water
but turn the pages of you.


2

In other places
I have been careful about intruders,
I have learnt about locks and iron bars.

Here I open a door
to admit a river, watch it spread across my floor
with palm seeds and the brittle claws
of crabs.

How often can you forgive me
for sinking your house
down to the secret bed of a river,
and for emerging from its wet dream
to embrace you with sudden spite,
like a lover?


3


I crush your fingers
like aromatic leaves
and hold them to my lips:
the fragrance of you fills me
and we dance on wet leaves
in a patch of sunlight
purer than the love you spoke to me.

And sunlight dances now
on the torn skirt of the river,
on the glistening rocks…
as my own love, like spilled blood,
swirls slowly to stillness
and fills the soft shallows,
the warm hollows
of the silence on the surface
of you.

4

After the body's shrill song
comes a silent love
like the calm reaches of a river
that earlier crashed down stone stairs,
its head boiling with foam and passion…
And you wonder:
"Was all of that for me?"

And you look beyond love
as a river, tasting salt
in its tidal mouth, stiffens
for the Judas-kiss of the sea;
finding no ground for hope,
you surrender silently to me
wondering, as you lose yourself in love,
"Will love still remember me?"


5

What is this love
we are always rehearsing?
Where will it take us
at the end of what day?

To whom do we offer
these arms and lips
and the hardened tips of ourselves
in mock surrender
— in rituals that sunder
stone and sky, cloud and thunder?

I try to remember
a reason for it all,
a grain of truth behind the gesture;
but truth is no longer to be found
where we have always sought her.
We grow too old for belief.
Like the sky, we simply shrug –
the stone's indifference to water.

6

Because rivers contain
the history of space,
I call you to come with me
into those amber shallows.

We start with creeks:
Kamuni, Wauna, Warapoka,
they become no more nor less
than your naked body,
which I enter to discover
– in that fluid mirror –
the past and the future
of my face.

Next the larger tributaries
Potaro, Cuyuni, Barama…
Ah, do not be fooled
by the contiguity of surfaces;
we descend into separate depths
where each river's cold is a different shiver,
and shattered light falls dully

into your drifting hair.
There is primordial memory there
in poured libations that are sufficient
to reach the spirit of the sea.

And Demerara, Corentyne, Waini:
I whistle for you across those estuaries;
my tears become the same salt as the sea.
I anchor myself to your vast body
raking the flesh of a continent
on the soft, forgetful beds of rivers,
making and healing
the scars of my race.


7


There are insects that crawl
on the skin of rivers,
giving you gooseflesh;
but the long brush of a hand
doesn't break your surface
on which I can still count the stars.

I watch the trees descending
to the sky, each with a blur
of unkept promises. I hear you sigh
like breeze on the flesh of the river;
cold fingers of mist caress you
and my body and I await
your subtle capitulations.

In this frenzy
of leaf-rot and sun-struck foam
I ease out of you,
lathered with your involuntary laughter,
nursing the crumpled remnant
of my story – now in danger
of abridgement in midstream…

I who must love rivers
love you too much
to succumb to your only dream.


8


Hearing the tidal beat of your wings
above the river, I look upward
to see the morning sky stained
with your brilliant love for me.

The noontide, swollen
with my faltering pride,
bears me beyond the reach
of your farthest tendril finger
and the cloudless sky consumes me.

Evening washes me back to your warmth,
across the groins of love's wide estuary;
and I imagine that I have turned your time
into the living flesh of memory.

Night severs the umbilical strand
of our love and I wait
in the tether of your throbbing tide
for the drowned touch of another dawn
to release me.


9


To take you
like a smooth river stone
to the hollow of my neck
is to dream of freedom
beyond the cool skin of ecstasy,
beyond fossil, beyond the finesse
of rhyme and memory.

To dream of loving you and rivers
has been to discover the specific thirst
of earth for sky
and the fragile patina of being
painted on the gifts of time.

10

When I finally rolled away
the stone of your love
that concealed the self I sought in rivers,
I was awakened to
                    sudden sorrow
by the cruel sunlight
streaming from an ordinary sky
through the startling absence
                    of you.

# MAZARUNI I
### (*For Paschal Jordan*)

I am silver in the afternoon,
mirroring the engine that sustains me –
I suppose it is my god,
insofar as I have one. I,
in turn, am divine to all that dwell
within me and sip life at my margins
to fashion other colours that contain me
– mostly green, though the softer
tissue of petal and ripe fruit can sport
whatever hue their bearers' codes
dictate. Purple is nice
and bright yellow. But green,
yellow or purple, all matter
that I enliven returns to me; I
dissolve their colours in me
yet I am not coloured by the colour
of any of them, but keep
my mirror polished to reflect
my lord of light and to obscure
the secrets of my depths. I guard
my own in darkness, even while
I shine with the image of my god:
I am Mazaruni, and I am silver
in the afternoon.

## APPROACHING KURUKABARU

*(In memory of Bernard Darke, S.J.)*

Like a finger caught in a trap
or a harp, the old Dakota
plucks the ragged strings
of light and shadow as it points
down to the smooth hills below.
Smooth hills make for bumpy air,
though, and as the ride roughens
towards its final flare before the touch
of earth, I was prompted to spare
a moment's imagining, a thought
for the loom and lurch
of the four last things.

The first is easiest, perhaps:
all poems are about Death,
the breath that sounds each syllable
carries death's dank fragrance
(despite the pleasures of rhyme)
and quivers, like this aeroplane,
on the edge of falter-
ing. The hills that rush up to meet us
could be the sacrificial altar
on which time's fullness spills
this whole basket, eggshell, brain —
all the worlds that might have succeeded
and will never come again...

Judgement is harder,
shoving everything towards measurement.
Accounting skills bore me
and talk of weights and balances

reminds me of shopkeepers
with a heavy thumb on the salt-beef,
diluting harsh calculation with whimsy
(and so redeeming the transaction – for me).
But one pays for it all in the end.
I look around surmising
who among us will rise, who descend
in the cruelty of the moment;
for it seems so harsh to make eternity
a creature of time, that mindless drudge:
the thought of Judgment is only bearable,
in the end, because one loves and trusts the judge.

Perhaps it was Hell
that ignited that plume of exhaust gases
behind the right engine.
"Nothing to worry about," the first officer said
with a chuckle… Hell might be
a place of knowing chuckles.
Perhaps we move always in
and out of Hell – as we now skim
these hills, dappled with sun and shadow,
getting near to an end.
Every convenient betrayal is its own sorrow
and Hell is wherever love hardens and dies,
like the cruel crush of earth
against this Pakaraima sky
we are trying to abandon.

I glimpse the plane's shadow,
cruciform on the hills of time
and all is suddenly redeemed;
as the wheels touch, Heaven might be
no more than these ancient sandstone hills,

fretted with watercourses
where the incomparable light leaps
at your eyes in an abandon of love.
Smoke rises like incense from thatched huts
and the pencilled paths across the hills
like stout cords bind this place
ever more tightly to your heart.

Beyond this destination
there are other destinations and still
another Destination.
As I watch you
take the inevitable photograph
and survey the path from here,
who can say whether it leads
to the unsheathed sword or the spiced wine?
Our only way is forward.

## MAZARUNI II

The wind-kissed river
breaks into ripples that flow
counter to the falling tide;
I dive into her restless side.
My body disappears for an instant
between swells like parallel ribs; I am
like a knife aimed at the river's heart.
Too soon I break the surface, leaving
her internal secrets undiscovered
like submerged eldorados.
She neither hurts nor bleeds
but buoys me with a gentleness
I take for love. "Rivers" – I read
in a scrawl of foam when I stand
on the bleached jetty again –
"rivers are drifting earth-clouds,
they are kin to sky and falling rain    "
But not to humans who dive,
looking for love or memories.

Rivers reject us – softly, perhaps,
but absolutely. I sit on the jetty
wet with you, Mazaruni, but
I prepare to plunge the blade
of my body into your side again,
in quest of the ancestral blood
of my belonging. "Vain," I hear you sigh,
"Entirely in vain…"

## SURFACE AND SURRENDER

It rained half the morning
in the heart that weighted your arrival,
until a brisk breeze from the south
drove before it a flurry
of leaves, like bills of lading,
and was permitted to remove
the sky's dark cargo of clouds...
With the washed day
now hung out in the sun to dry,
a white monogrammed handkerchief
fluttered out of the downriver trees
and grew into the solid bulk of the steamer...
As the sailors took up the slack
on the stern hawser,
I saw you emerge on deck:
the morning and the evening
of my new-blown day.

When you sat on the grey-painted capstan
in your white dress,
your sleeveless arms reminding the sun
of the texture of longing,
I felt with a sudden thrill
how superfluous to the moment
was the tide of my blood
or the green flash of your eyes
and yet the signatures
of such anatomical intimacies
are what I can still read so clearly,
long after the triumph of time.

On the stelling you confessed to me:
"I slept with the rain",
and when I looked to the river for signs of betrayal
the rippled laughter of sunlight
distracted me from the depths of your passion;
trapped on the surface of doubt
like the shadow of a passing cloud,
I — as always — surrendered, and the moment
was so transformed by the glow
of your flesh that the idle boys
sitting on the bollards caught the scent
of rain and the storm that brewed beneath the breath
of each phrase we spoke:
"So you slept with the rain, so
where does that leave us?"
— "It *unleaves* us, as any good storm would",
and our bare limbs twined together
in the blast and we were bent upon love
and bent double by the power of love
and collapsed on the wet afternoon
like old trees fallen into the river...

When I left you at your father's house
I went back to the river, guilty
with an old secret passion — and envious;
you could say without fear, "I slept
with the rain", but I could never speak
of my love of the river
and how I let her mistress my lost body
in ways beyond wonder...

I tell myself you are the surface of my love,
and she the dark depth, and it rains all evening
as I await the consequences
of truths I did not fashion.

If an island is surrounded by river,
what authority causes it to resist
the river's restless motion? And why
would a river so perfectly define an island
only to have it subvert that river's
basic nature? There are real mysteries here.
Sand and soil the river sweeps along, silting
its own veins and channels, like
a shameless glutton fattening his own heart
— but islands refuse to budge,
they cause rivers, like Mazaruni,
to stumble and foam with rage
and to race through narrow, rocky channels,
muttering at the indignity. But
what do I know? That might be
the river's real pleasure — its secret vice
— getting its blood to race and thrum
until the rhythmic shudder
of its cataracts and falls
can sustain its stiff
tumescence
all the long, rippling way down,
down to the soft, dissolving sweetness
of the sea. Do I hear you chuckle darkly
among roots and rocks on the river bank?
Aha! I catch you! You, Mazaruni!

# A TRIPTYCH FOR WINTER

*(For Caroline Morgan Di Giovanni, and in memory of "Graffiti")*

1 *Icicles*

Icicles pending from the cabin roof
Winter's stiff dazzling pride
and sun-drip of the weary days, frozen
in mid-stride
and wavy with the wind.
Healed under the scab of night
they gloom cloudily at
the late homecomer with arms of wood
or the wide-wandering scavenger of dark.
But all things recreate themselves
– even in winter, so
the next day's festering sun will rise
to lubricate with its light
those glittering phalloi of the season
until they drip their life onto the prophylactic snow,
spawning stunted, frozen, inverted icicles
standing precisely in line, far below…

2 *Conversation across a Winter Pond*

"Tonight" – the word fluttered across the crystal space
over the frozen pond, over the horizon of hope,
to be snagged, perhaps, in a strand
of her wind-tossed hair as she stood, twinkling
in the distance, like a star…
A blue-blur of icicle-voice
and new whispers on the fibbing wind:

"No" — and she moved; slow
to trap the sound, I fed an ear
to the numbing blast, then a muffled "Please"
answered only by a headshake
down the bluster of the breeze.
She seemed as planted and unmovable
as the trees. "Why not?" — or just "Why?"
Again the frozen wind was thieving words from me;
even gestures blurred in the bitter cold:
a nod of her head was as negative
as the ice-distance, as I left her standing
in the snow-smoke and the captive sky
on the other side of all my longing... and turned
towards the cabin. Winter teaches how to die.


3  *The Snow-Giver*

[*He gives snow like wool; he scatters hoar frost like ashes
— Psalm 147*]

The hunter
came upon the cabin,
quiet, half-
under the snow.

His eye was sad
and his pace,
approaching,
was slow.

The burnt-out hearts
no longer beat,
frozen, but
did the hunter
know?

The cabin seemed empty,
empty, so he passed;
love left no
footprints in the
snow.

# MAZARUNI IV

In the evening, and in the overhang
of trees, you can see that I am
a black river; but be careful what
you read into my colour – I know
you poets and the irresponsibility
of your traffic in tropes and symbols.
Don't you dare discover in my blackness
the hubris of racial solidarity!
I am no kin to the hue of humans
(nor the "you" of youth, nor the "with"
of withered old age; there is no part of speech
that can forge identity between me and you).
I do not share your ethnocentric dreams,
for my blackness is not inherited: clear
and colourless are my ancestral mountain streams.

I am black because of what I carry – and
I don't mean the sins of man or nature;
mine is not that moral darkness that
you oppose to the light and the love of God,
but simply the chemistry of leaf and bark
in water, and the need to keep my bowels
free from clogging weeds that feed
upon the sunlight. I am black for my own
protection, and to make myself inscrutable
to prying poets like you, who, in trying
to expose my depths and secrets, would
convey only a point of view – a moment
and a place caught like a fish in a brief
basket of lethal exposure, doomed
to fade and die.

I was before the first anchor
of human thought broke the surface
of any stream, seeking the purchase of love;
and I will be when only anchors remain,
like rusted runes in layers of river stone.
I am Mazaruni, and I am always alone.

# WORDS AGAINST TIME

Whenever, in the naked dark,
that deepest silence beyond time
threatens to overshadow us,
we seek to break its fearful spell
by speaking words of love and lust
to insulate us from the past
and keep us safe from rote and rust.

Then, through the warmth of your breast
I can feel the words of you
beating like huge wing'd birds,
as the bars of their living cage
press against my nakedness.

Then I reach and touch you
where the cage is flimsiest,
and the warm, feathery wonder
of you leaps against my hand,
and in the shadow of time's ampersand
we tumble into wordlessness...

# MAZARUNI V

You are thinking of time and rivers
but what you seek to know you falsify.
We are both elusive, time and I. You
name me "Mazaruni", but what you see
or feel is only a simulacrum of my being.
At the next turn of tide it will be gone,
yet what you continue to see will be
as much of me as you will ever know.
The river you enter now, your body
lathered with soap, is what time calls
"history", and will be stuck in your memory,
your imagination of rivers. But
when you recall it, you recall
other than me. I am always and irretrievably
now and now and now, no "then",
no "will be". Except inside your head,
where the experience of me is altered
at its edges, the way my passing
alters islands and river banks. In time
you will perhaps be pleased to discover
that my substance and my ceaseless flow,
within your mind's eye, will have subtly
altered the person you imagine yourself to be.

## THE TROUBLE WITH ENGLISH B*
*(After listening to a group of 5<sup>th</sup> formers preparing for the exam)*
*(For Keith Noel)*

Is that you can never be sure
how you've done; I mean teachers
have too much leeway to judge; they won't
tell you what a poem means
nor *exactly* what a hero is –
after all, they're supposed to know...

We were given a poem to analyse the other day:
"It's about ripeness," I wrote,
the yellows, the browns, the maturity
of the season..." My best friend wrote:
"It's about death; the yellows, the browns,
the fruit on the ground..."
"You were both right," the teacher said,
giving us each seventeen out of twenty
and all the teeth of her smile.
But how could he be right
if I am right: ripeness
is not the same as death,
they even have different smells...

It's all because of words –
in the dictionary they're OK,
tied firmly to meaning, like
Miss Redman goat staked out in the grass-piece:
they know their place – in the dictionary.
But put them in a story
or a poem, and they get on so wild
it make you shame. Words in literature
remind me of two well-known girls
in our fifth form:

they kiss around with all the boys
and tell each one what he wants to hear —
might be exciting but you can't
*respect* them. I have no respect
for English B, for sluttish words
that would lift their skirts for anybody...

In maths the square root of forty-nine
is always seven: every time
you work it out the answer is the same;
if you get six or eight you wrong,
no arguments, no alternative readings,
no "this is how it makes me feel".
I like that: faithfulness, consistency
predictability, exactness. The world
needs more of these...

And don't talk about Shakespeare:
instead of simply saying "young man" or "adolescent"
we have to struggle with "a squash
before 'tis a peascod" and "a codling
when 'tis almost an apple" — too
many unknown, unreliable words
to deal with, causing bare confusion
in Caribbean schools where nobody
never seen a peascod, and I always thought
a codling was that false prick them old-time men
used to strap on to impress the women...
And that duke got to be some kind of buller
to fall in love with a girl dressed up as a boy...
How can anyone write sense in an exam
about such foolishness...?

* English B is the literature syllabus of the regional CSEC examinations
administered by the Caribbean Examinations Council.

# CLAIRVOYANCE

I will die in the hills of south-
western Pennsylvania, on a day made darker
by the overhanging trees. A day without breeze.
I will fold into the forest
not far from the highway
where the appalled squirrels will scurry away,
leaving a silence perfect for dying.

That evening the moon will leak
through bleak foliage and illuminate
half of my face, a hand and the exposed ankle
of one leg. And not far away to the west
the silence of the Ohio river
will be broken by shrill moonlight
and lovers will thrill to moments
that have no memory of me.

I will die in the hills
of south-western Pennsylvania.

# TOMORROW AND THE CHILDREN
*(For Amparo)*

Sometimes I look at my hands
the hands that wield pen and laser pointer
that cup your rounded breasts
that chop garlic and green onions
that strive to aim carefully when peeing
in the midnight darkness
that gesture forlornly to an inconvenient lover
that rip the insides out of hope
and then quickly stop a tear in its track
that reach between my own shirt buttons
trying to remember the warmth of flesh
that clasp resignedly behind my back
that love the smooth lightness of your hair
that push the river water in powerful strokes
aiming for the safety of the raft of logs
across from the sawmill,,, that turn red
with the blood of berries in season
that tickle your armpits, that cover your eyes
in childish playfulness, that cover my ears
to deafen your chiding response:
"For chrissake, when will you grow up?"
that plunge into wave-churned sand
to retrieve the fallen wedding ring
before it disappears, that melt the ice
of your toes on wintry evenings and test
the fire of your forehead in times of fever…

These same hands that wield pen and laser pointer
now reach out for tomorrow and the children.

III

THE MUSEUM OF LOVE

# RAIN BEFORE DAWN
## *(For Amparo)*

This morning, before the first hint of sunrise,
rain, driven by a stiff breeze,
came through the bedroom window
and wet us awake.

It happens all the time:
the routine is to leap out of bed
and wind the louvres shut.
But this time some perversity
born of the dregs of a common dream,
perhaps, made us lie still
and be lashed by the rain.

The cloud quickly passed
— or the wind died —
and the louvres remained open wide.

Then you turned your wet nakedness towards me,
looking perhaps for warmth,
and found that familiar accommodation
of flesh knowing and accepting its other self.
The rain-wetness added an exciting *glissade*
to the old movements
and stirred a depth of mutual passion
scarcely plumbed before
in sixteen years of marriage.

So our bodies surprise ourselves
with that miracle of rediscovery
that is possible only after long cohabitation.

In the first grey bloom of the new day
you continue to hold me tight within you
and my tears of wonder replace
the blessed drops of rain upon your face.

# TIME
## (For Ian McDonald)

Time tunnels us all
like a weevil
in a grain of rice,
leaving us hollow,
unmarrowed,
a shell full of memory...
But is time nourished
by what it digests
of our youth and substance?
Perhaps we need
to know museums
before we become them:
to hear our own
footsteps echo
in the quiet corridors,
as we search the contents
of the stomach of time
in order to re-
discover the truth
that once flashed
in our laughing eyes.

# THE MUSEUM OF LOVE   I

*(For Ted and Lorna)*

The speaking voice is the spirit of a young boy born into the last years
of plantation slavery who was shot dead in a mango tree (mistaken for
a monkey – according to the manager who shot him from the window
of the great house); this spirit lives in the museum where it has attached
itself to the wooden sculpture of a black boy. The ragamuffin and his
followers are the restless spirits of murdered street urchins that take
refuge in the museum at night and continue to visit their mischief and
waste and violence on the silent but numinous world of art and artefact.


There were times when I longed
to be like the ragamuffin,
a jack in patched pants and
the rip and flutter of shirt-tail,
and hard, untidy hair, grin and
skinteeth to hide discomfort, while
all I had was nakedskin and helpless tears
("my mummy!"), no longer free to wander,
only to wait, to want in secret. At six o'clock
they close the doors and my dark
polished wood-world keeps me awake
with sad dreams: "I want my mummy!"

I dream her in the next room
wrapped tight in dry banana leaves,
all her succulent mother-love dried to dust
and crumble, and silent sighs
not even the alarm can detect.
But I can hear her silence;
she calls to me over the ocean of
empty floor, under which my fathers
and their fathers' fathers float

like polished dreams down corridors
and middle passages. Below, the guard
plies his soft boots of history,
overloaded with feet and yards and miles,
the distances between here and home and hope.
"I love you, Son!" and "I love
you, Mother!" criss-and-cross the ocean floor
like the shadows of birds, like
the colours of oil on water, like the
crab-crawled books and beaches
of my untold, untellable story, like you, visitor,
too preoccupied with what you call life;
you stare at me and take my black shadow
into the pale panic of your dreams...

We saw this boy, Mummy, a brown
ragamuffin, a spirit, though not like us;
he's unattuned to museum time and un-
attached to any ancient tool or artefact —
has no fixed place among us.
He leads a group of urchin spirits
from the real city of flesh and pain.
He was news the first time he came
among us; I dreamt he dreamt me
and drowned me in the wither
of his wander and his waste of breath...
It's no use talking to them, Mummy,
he just laughs, skins his rotten teeth
and wipes my words like dribble
with the back of his hand. He loves
the lobes and tubers of the land he lives;
and all the other children nibble
at the knub of his hand and
are fed deep on his museum secrets

and treasures; and his mummies wake and dance
and they clap and clown and cloud
the face of his frown and he shouts:
"Silence!" and they Shhhhh and are
silent. And Shhh and whisss and ummm
and "Silence!" and "That is all we ever own",
he says, and shoves words down our throats
to silence us and to sign us, in the name
of the humm of the mummy and the lonely
ghosts."

# ELF-PORTRAIT

*Adieu! The fancy cannot cheat so well*
*As she is famed to do, deceiving elf...*

As a child he had size and stature;
vast as estuaries, he was that riparian aristocrat
whose alluvial accent sounded in the bedrooms of all rivers.

Now time has shrunk him to a smooth homunculus, a dwarf
among men, his appetite for adventure channelled
into dusty classrooms and suburban homes.

Marriage has tamed his vagabond lust. He has now
no interesting conversation,
no knowledge of political scandals or other labyrinths.

What he does have are memories —
stuffed with them: priapic memories of river-maids,
river-spirits and the palpable gods of mud-flats and forests.

But gods and forests are fled into ideas,
they have lost their giant stature,
have shrunk to match his world's diminishment...

In some bleak future they will say,
"He's quite mad now (you know): a limp exile
looking endlessly over the restless sea,

dreaming aloud,
and talking in tedious verse
about teaching the rivers to sing!"

# THE MUSEUM OF LOVE  II

Museums are cold at night
when the wake of my cries, crossing
the floor of the Egyptian gallery, fainter
than the smudge of moonlight through dusty
windows, warns of subtly tactile thoughts
despite "Do not touch the exhibits" and
the fierce frown of the grey guard, draped
in all the centuries of my sorrow ("Mummy!");
and when his back is turned, like a traitor
the floor sighs relief and my dream advances
under the cover of night, of numbness, of not...
In my dream the ragamuffin reaches
into a torn trouser pocket and produces
a thin knife – flick-and-open – and a thin
blade's inserted between the banana leaves
of the book of your body, grazing
your imagined ribs, and his eyes flash
and the knife flashes when he closes it.
"Mummy!", and "Murder!" I shout to the guard,
and "Murder!", inaudible to all but the dead,
echoes faintly through the halls; and
the blood of your love rises in the rinse
of reflections from polished floors, in the
hinged whisper of tired doors, in the mute
mumble of the shuffle of lost feet,
and the crime, like all the crimes
of my fathers' flesh, settles into the sleep
of the museum city. The clocks strike
and it is another foreday morning of the rust
on the rim of the rest of my unborn life.

# FOUR VARIATIONS ON THE THEME
## OF INDEPENDENCE I

*(For Pat Symmonds)*

At the time
none of us could foresee
the choked highways nor the rise in crime —
our senses too full of the comforting smoke
of burning empire,
and the political sublime
of smugly squandered words
spent to ease our nervous climb
up to the floodlit podium
to bow before the world.

And now
the world is no longer amused
at our miniature gestures
of pleading or of pain,
refracted again and again
in all these splinters of islands
that pierce our tourist-brochure sea.

If you ask me
it's time we tune and trim
this prodigal independence
(in Guyana, TT, Bim)
time we get together and learn to swear
in one loud choral voice
        big bad words that the world
will have to hear.

# THE MUSEUM OF LOVE  III

It was the day that Mac first came
into the museum of my memory,
came in a group from school, a coffle
of chained spirits, whispering because of the
polish, the teacher, the guards, the loud silence.
Mac was the most beautiful of them all,
her worthless flesh easily outshone
the priceless treasures, the debris of past
worlds, and no artefact could match her wide
brown smile or the bare, clipboard-hugging
arms whose magic circle I would die
a thousand times again to enter...
Mac was the life I could barely remember,
the warmth of breath, the body-smell
beneath the smells of pencil shavings
and the carnal rubbings of erasers. Her clear,
brown eyes looked full on all of us dead
and dared the dust of our hearts to remember
the ache and flutter of love.

The memory of a heart in me woke
with sudden hurt from the heretic ages
and a stab or spasm beyond the whittle of wood,
beyond the black sentence of my carved features,
beyond my adopted name of artefact, shook
me from pate to pedestal, like the sudden shout
from the corridor: "Immaculata!
Please try to keep up with the class and do
stop daydreaming..." And she suddenly started
as I shook, or was it I? Or was it

she? Or was it who? Who shook the moment
of our meeting of eyes and set the scene for all
our future disturbance, dream and dalliance?
I saw her shiver and retrieve her now,
her nonce, her notion of lifeless wood,
I saw her eyes judge me, Mummy, and she
sucked the teeth of her gnawing doubt and
she turned and left me love. And love swelled
my wooden moment into a dream of living trees,
into leaf and bark and blossom and the memory
of veined water under a black skin, keeping
me cool... My Immaculata...

# VARIATIONS ON THE THEME OF INDEPENDENCE II
*(For Esther Phillips)*

Independence is a cat on the sofa:
ask him kindly to get down
and see the look he gives you;
is the house-guest
who came "for a brief stay"
which has now outlasted your patience,
your humour and your stocks of Mount Gay,
as he holds you captive to his endless conversation.

Independence is that sleek multinational
parked on the edge of your labour laws,
ready to start his flawless engine
at the first sign of polite remonstration
and hit the road for a friendlier town;
leaving you standing, astonished,
in his exhaust: a blue puff of calumny
just strong enough to spook
his fellow-travellers and their hard currency.

Independence is that wise trading partner
who gives fatherly advice
on how to vote at the U.N.;
who will warn his vacationing countrymen
about crime and other dangers in your land
unless you let him hold your hand
and fondle your soft developing market
with his prurient TV commercials…
and you shouldn't say "cultural rape",
it's just the intricacies of trade,
you must understand…

Independence is that annual visitor
or quasi-diplomat who explores your island
in his CD jeep or rented car, who
knows its lore and its history better than you
and repeats it loudly to newcomers
in your best restaurants.
"Independence" is the name of the house
he will build, after retirement, on your prime beach land...
And the question is: if he hires you
to cook his meals or cut his grass
will his independence and your independence
become the same thing at last?

My soul ached for the lost root of home
and the bark of the raw ribs of the dog
rooting the night for food or love or the spirit of place
and the howl of the moon and the breeze
through the stiffening hackles of fear
as the tall trees moan, and in the big house
the man with the gun twitches in his rum-
assisted sleep next to the naked shiver of girl
he had called from the kitchen hut to weave the web
of missing wife – in England buying hats...
All these stories, this store of lore, I learned in
the airless warmth of the hut in those nights
of uncles, when I  turned my face to the wall
and kept as quiet as this museum, though
I longed to be alone with you then, as I
long for you now, Mummy...

But that night the ragamuffin stalked
like a dream through the drift of vague
suspicions and the faint musk of Mac's moment
before the black wood of my prison; he
traversed the dream of our love, I could tell,
but his heart, like the bright blade of his knife,
could read only "seize", "sunder" and "sever"
and his careless stamp of bewilderment,
his involuntary "Huh" of suspicion summoned
the grizzled guard from below the decks
of fallen cards, like my fathers' ghosts,
and his running shoes pinned the mask
of fear on Ragamuffin's face, and I felt
sorry for him, for his life on knife-edge,
for his ancient, squalid murder of my mother...

Sorry, and his eyes softened in the gloom
and he melted down the corridor of my pity
leaving the puffing heart of the old guard empty,
except for the hoax of beating blood
that pounded in his ears like a stamping heel
or the "Huh" of voiceless fears of delusion...

# VARIATIONS ON THE THEME OF INDEPENDENCE III
### (*In memory of Alfred Pragnell*)

When the telephone wake her
at three o'clock in the morning
to say Cossie in hospital because somebody
stab he outside a rum shop in St. George,
she couldn't say she was surprised,
though she dress same time, call taxi
and find herself down QEH
as if she was a dutiful, loving wife...

He never regain consciousness
and by the time the frail kite-string
of his life slip through his hand
four days later on that hospital bed,
it was as if he dead long, long ago:
all she could remember was
the pain that man bring her,
the blows when he come home drunk,
the shame when he turn up drunk
at the bakery, waving a broken bottle
and demanding to see "that bitch ah does
live wid, who ent cook no food
for de man for two whole days."
Then there was the fat girl from Redman village
and the fat girl from Charo Bridge,
and all the other fat girls he used to make sure she know about —
just because she was slim
and tried to have a little dignity...

Up to now she ent cry no tears.
The day after the funeral she pack up
all his things in one medium-size cardboard box

(his whole life fit in one cardboard box)
and take it to his sister.
Then she go home, cross road
and beach and walk into the sea
in all her clothes.

She splash water on her head,
she throw water up in the air,
she duck into a wave.
The sea water feel cool and clean
and she remember watching people get baptize
on that same beach. Walking back up
the sand, she feel free, she feel light
despite the heavy wet clothes.
The neighbours come running up, looking worried:
"Girl, you alright?"
"Don't let this trouble make you do anything foolish."
"God, I get so frighten – the children
say you trying to drown yourself."

She laugh and laugh and she spin round
showering them with water from her hair
and the full bloom of her wet skirt.
"Drown myself? Not me, Darling,
I celebrating.
I celebrating independence day."

Mac returned the next day; I heard her laughter
in distant corridors ages before she burst
like long forgotten sunlight into my fiction
of real presence. I was her project, she told
her friend, as she stooped to copy the words
on my plaque: "Sculpture of African Boy.
Artist unknown – almost certainly a plantation slave –
early nineteenth century." I watched the curve
of her neck as she wrote, I longed for nape
and nuzzle – the living smell of her hair, her
bitten lower lip, the throb and twitch
of her concentration… Suddenly she stood
and looked at me, not at my face… she looked
furtively around and then I saw her friend's
gum-chewing lower jaw fall open, then I felt it!
She touched my willie! that miserable shrimp
of black wood that I had long forgotten
to be ashamed of – till that moment. "Mac,
they say don't touch – O God, Mac – you
touched him *there*!" and her friend laughed
from behind a muffling hand and Mac smiled
and looked around again. "It's small", she said,
"but nice and hard". They both giggled and I knew
then that she was my own love for ever and ever,
Mummy…

# VARIATIONS ON THE THEME OF INDEPENDENCE: IV
## (*For Tony Kellman*)

It is never the official shout of freedom
that makes you free.  Freedom,
like love, is not reducible to a seminal act.

You would think that with our history
we would be wary of declarations,
of days that promise to transform our lives.
Emancipation, Adult Suffrage, Independence –
liberation after liberation and how many more
to come, bearing their impossible promises
so insistently that they wring
our reluctant hearts into glad acquiescence
for the moment, for the day.
Who does not love a celebration,
the dispensation of honours,
the self-annunciation of a new people
– who are yet the old people
celebrating freedom for the first and the repeated time…?

What if freedom,
like the slime of gutters,
is too far beneath our pride?
What if we prefer to hide
in the smug labyrinth of
freedom as artefact, as gift,
as politician's favour – something
that smells and tastes like us?
What if, by celebrating the day,
we are worshipping its father, Time,
and not the maker of time?
What if freedom belongs to no one?
What if it was ours all the time?

# READING INDEPENDENCE DAY, BARBADOS
*(For Kamau)*

When I open the text of *Independence Day*,
as usual I skip the official blather
in the front, not bothering to look for
familiar names in the epistles dedicatory;
I flip past the tedious parades
of important citizens in upper case bold –
theirs is a story too often told
to captive school children and the assembled ranks
of those faithful to all the forms,
now receiving their official "thanks".

Instead I find, in some small middle chapter,
the empty beach of a page
with a slender column of writing
down one side, like a Brathwaite poem,
like a fringe of trees behind the naked
sand and the lapping waves.
Independence morning:
the children come dancing
down and imprinting with their feet and hands
the joy of a holiday in the sand;
the dragged cricket bat, the surfboard's skeg,
the old dinghy's battered keel
all cut the name of freedom
into memories I can feel...

I leaf past pompous buildings
festooned with fading bunting
that won't come down until it's time
for the Christmas lights;

I avoid the television's formal frown
and the jingoistic delights
of the pages of National Culture...

I find instead a lonely paragraph
near North Point, on sea cliffs
where I hear through my planted feet
the primordial boom and shock
of the clash between eternal wave and rock –
the same as was heard
by Arawak, by planter and by slave
arriving at this end of their island's tether...
I delight in the imagined echoes
of their passing, now mingled together
in the deep mutter of the undermining sea;
I savour its comforting, ironic harmony
on this two thousandth-and-whatever page
of the guilt and glitter of history.

I leaf along the north-east coast
not noticing the paper-cut from Pico Teneriffe
until the salt spray stings
near the pages of Cattlewash. There
I find the sand's wide palimpsest
inscribed at evening with a single trail
of footprints beside a strange, sinuous hieroglyph –
as if a sea-serpent and its master
had passed that way.
Further along the mystery is solved:
I come upon a lone reef-fisherman
dragging in the sand his metal spear
on which is impaled a cluster of sea-cats.
He heads home into the evening glow
of his own ageless contentment.

It is time. I too must go,
follow the sun across those ancient hills.
As I drive through the familiar clauses,
the intimate winds and hollows of the centre,
I am ambushed by sudden tears
(perhaps the setting sun in my eyes?)
and that fierce love for this adopted rock of home
that redeems the official cliché
as I close the book:
My freedom. My Independence day.

But that night (O God, Mummy),
that same sleepless night after Mac
had become the love beyond my life,
late that night, when the moon
was loud on the polished floorboards,
and the guards had lapsed into that inertia
indistinguishable from sleep, and our own
night conversations across the galleries
had faded… the ragamuffin came
and stood in front of me. I tried,
Mummy, I tried to hide my secret,
but he looked at me and he *knew*
and "Hah!", he said, in the voice
of the man with the gun, in the voice
of the night-uncles, in the voice
of the dozing guards, in the voice
of all those who discover transgressions·
"HAH!", and he flicked open his knife
faster than my wooden eyes could see
and in a flash he chopped off
my little wooden willie, cutting
against the grain of all my hope,
castrating my dream of love and laughter,
of the awakening of wood to the life
of trees, swaying in the breeze, to the
flow of sap and water and blood and tears…
and he slipped the curled shrimp of wood
with the flick-knife into his pocket.

Then he showed me all the rotten teeth
of his grin: "Hah, you museum creatures
have all the time in the world for desire,

but not the means, not the flesh, not
the blood, not the real presence…
I won't let you forget that, like me,
you are all victims of the murder of love…"
And all I could think of, Mummy,
was the look of shock on her face
when Mac would come the next time –
and to think that in life, in death
and forever after death I will know
no love, Mummy, it broke my wooden heart…

# FLOTSAM: FRAGMENT OF A SEA FAN
## (*For Edward Baugh*)

A skeletal hand
with obscene extra fingers
dredged from the bottom of the sea
where it plucked the rhythmic strings
of swift tidal guitars
and made music for all
the drowned kin of our memory...

At the same time
it gestured rudely at passing ships
(middle finger for the middle passage)
lost for three hundred years
and webbed with the complex memories
of flesh scarcely more solid than water
now bleached greyish white
to confound old massa and new
black masters too, who
might want to claim allegiance...

All it seeks now
is silent oblivion,
but we put it on view:
the ocean's sculpted, ancestral waste
becomes a curiosity on a shelf
speaking to us of drowned places
and whispering in soft, sad silence
about the fragile structure of self.

## RITES OF SPRING
### (For Carolyn Cooper)

Arriving in mid-afternoon
and waiting for check-in time,
I find the Nassau hotel's pool area
infested with American kids on spring break.
From behind glass in the adjacent dining room
I observe as the frothy tequila concoction
they consume (as though life depended upon it)
gradually raises the volume of their youthful voices;
their gestures grow more emphatic, their faces
flushed... the way they touch each other
becomes less circumspect and more urgent –
like desperate love – as the blender mug
full of their happiness arrives yet again
through the doorway of a nearby ground-floor room...
Perhaps it's an important post-adolescent rite
that I should not be witnessing... That night
the noise invades our hotel bedrooms as they sing,
sounding now like drunken sports fanatics
yelling for their side's – or any side's – victory.
In the wee hours they abandon all inhibitions, leaping
into the pool, pulling off each other's clothes, insisting
that all get naked – like truth, perhaps, like their gifts
of time and youth, like the already fading memory
of a heart that can feel, without the erasure
of drunkenness, all the wild wonder of the world...

The scene from my balcony, four floors above,
reminds me of a Titian painting (I can't recall
the name) where young people, much like these,
cavort in a rustic setting, with Bacchus sprawled

senseless somewhere in the background, and a
tipsy toddler, lifting his chemise, pisses delightedly
into the stream of wine (I was suddenly gripped
by the thought of these revellers giving new meaning
to "the wee hours", and resolved to avoid the pool this trip…)

In the surrounding hotel rooms
serious conference delegates (like me)
toss in their fragile sleep, mumbling profanities
at the kids and their infernal noise. But aren't we
here too for our own rite of spring? Our dull
academic papers purchasing a few days
of conviviality: the delirium of a brief escape
from the routine. It's only that, with the help
of careful language and other learned refinements,
we manage our excesses more discreetly –
our boisterousness emerging in wild dancing
on the last night at the Dean's reception,
or in peevish comments we feel we have to make
during a colleague's lengthy presentation…
Yet when we see how these spring-breakers bask
in the wild innocence that clings to them so sweetly,
our stern disapproval (like this poem) masks
the wistful longing that we feel — though not completely.

# THE MANAGER OF THE SAWMILL REMONSTRATES
## WITH HIS WIFE

### 1: *River and Rocks*

I hear the river complain loudly
about those rocks that would block its way
as it forces itself around and between,
spitting in their faces before
smoothing its black skin
for the remaining miles of the journey.

Such is the power I long for:
to flow and shout and have my way
despite all recalcitrance; but I
feel instead like the river rocks:
silent and sullen and spat upon
– and massively, embarrassingly *there*
in the middle of your life.

### 2: *A Burning Question*

Between my what and my why
hangs a third question,
hot, glistening and tumid,
which you have made me withdraw
to await your considered response.
I'm afraid that's no solution, Dear,
for my question has become a problem
that *you* can walk away from:
*I* can't: it walks with me
– or before me, or beneath me –

until its throbbing pain
infects my very soul...
while you enact domestic irrelevancies
within sight of my agony.
No point in polite talking any more,
let me write — inscribe my many years
of frustration — if not upon your flesh
with hard, appropriate instrument, then here
on paper with perhaps too fine a point.
The point, Love, is *love*.
Let me... Let me! Or accept
responsibility for the devastation
when the log-jam finally clears.


3: *Refusal*


Refusal is hard to bear
when there is no alternative.
My mind accepts all the valid reasons
yet cannot be at peace, for I —
who am, unfortunately, more than mind —
am not at peace, cannot resign
to nothingness, to not, to no...
Imagine a huge mora log that burst
the chains as it is hauled up the ramp:
there is too much substance
to be dragged back to rational control
from the brink of promised ecstasy;
it is impossible to dwell or linger
on such a brink. My bodily weight
demands a fall — either forward
or back. In the one case
the satisfaction will be physical

but in the other the injury is mental.
I grow tired of mental suffering.
Banish my misery (only you can)
and if you can't spare me your whole body,
then how about a helping hand?

IV

LE REPENTIR

# EMPYREAN

When life is haunted by fire
and one is branded, broiled, burnt,
the empyrean blooms
like an intuitive flower in a mind
accustomed to sheltering secrets
while searching everywhere for the cool touch,
the warm, gregarious comfort of love...
But love, too, catches fire
and I retreat when it roars in my ears;
and the most that I am permitted is to flinch
and offer a sacrificial hand for the flames.

So now I know
that all the ice on earth
can never cool that burning sphere,
nor negate all those cruel circumstances
where hopes quail like balsam leaves,
where the flesh of my imagination catches fire
and the residue of all life and love
is just a dry sweeping of dust,
a light film that barely darkens
the subjects of my desire...
yet serves a stern warning
about the impossibility of intimacy
and the eternal homelessness of my heart.

# THE PALMS OF *LE REPENTIR*

The magnificent palms
in *Le Repentir*
strut beside the daystream of the living,
ushering a city
through the quiet corner of its dead.

Their shadows lengthen over tombs
in the evening.

At night they harbour the spirits
of those buried there:
our long dead fathers, standing in line
as men here have always stood,
waiting... And the women:
they too are dredged nightly
from the river-beds of memory
to flaunt their style
in the impenetrable shade of the palms –
fragile in lace, or massive
in the sackcloth of my conscience –
mothers, all of them,
their endless commandments
now leaking through the fissures of their flesh
into the swamp.

In the morning all is peace
as the palms rock their heads
of sungilt leaves and mock
the fears of life and death
that wring us to repentance...
They have no such needs
as they rejoice in ecstasies of breeze

and morning dew at their planted feet
and are drunk, drunk deep of the seas
of purest sky-blue —
those great sentinel trees
of my memory.

## APPROACHING LE REPENTIR I
### *Pierre Louis De Saffon*

My heart raced as I ran
and knelt next to the fallen heap
that was my brother, the weapon
still smoking in my trembling hand...

I saw only a great surprise, no sign
of hatred in his dying eyes.
I lifted his head; he held my arm
and tried to speak, but only a faint
rattle and a shocking foam of blood
issued from between the pale lips...

"Forgive me!" I cried again and again
in desperation and thought I felt a faint
squeeze of his hand around my wrist;
I tried to look again into his eyes
but could see that they saw nothing,
not me, not the misty morning sky,
not the appalled seconds standing by –
nor heard he then my frantic, pleading cry.

It was the day my brother died
it was the day I had to die
to all but sorrow, penitence and shame...
And then that bottomless ship
and the heat and sweat and stink of Demerara...
Forgive me brother, forgive me God,
A man reduced to nothing but a name...

## A BAT AT DUSK
*(For Stewart Brown)*

Quietly, at dusk,
a bat emerges
from the corner of my eye
and I think I see him
rip an unworthy thought to shreds
using the last snagged rag of it
to whip himself higher
into the steel-grey vault of sky;
there he examines the emotional freight
of coming night – darting between the bales
of primitive fears like a customs clerk,
officious, driven –
telling in the thickening air
the costs of secreted luxuries:
sexual fantasies, imaginary feasts,
the delirium of heaven . . .

But when I looked hard,
trying to see the sum
of his final accounting,
I find he has merged his smooth black
into the whole dark cargo
of my mind, become my greatest fear,
as I sense the faint flash of tiny teeth
grinning behind the eyes
that can no longer see him.

## APPROACHING *LE REPENTIR* II
### *Plantation of Grief*

At first my spirit revolted against the place,
its physical assaults: the heat, the smell,
the mould-begetting damp, and all those creatures
that crawl under my skin to sting, or
bloom into red rashes and pustules,
itching souvenirs of the *tristes tropiques*...
Yet all these were not as burdensome
as that mental blight I brought with me from
France: the unshriven guilt of fratricide
weighed like a heavy seal upon my spirit which,
according to my beliefs and calculations,
I had already bequeathed to the devil...

But it is strange how the daily routine
and the necessary transactions of ordinary living
can anaesthetize hurt and cover the deepest scars
so that one becomes a familiar, harmless presence
to neighbours and others — if not yet to the self.
As I served more time I learnt to embrace
the spirit of this devil of a place, and especially
the business of plantations that produced
the world's sweetest substance
from its most bitter cruelties. As a slave
to my sinful act, I considered my own fate worse
than that of the plantation slaves, despite
the whip, the withering word, the wild caprice
of men like me who conspired to make
the system profitable... the slaves were free
from guilt and I could never be.

I learnt the business well, believing in
the natural ascendancy of my race and
the entitlement to status and comfort that
not even the unlawful killing of a brother
could erase. I acquired what the world calls wealth;
I invested in my own plantations, distinguishing
them with the names I chose, through which
to channel my lifelong guilt and grief: *La Penitence*
and *Le Repentir*: names that I bequeath like scars
to be worn forever on this soft earth, to signify
a sorrow without relief... My plantations of grief.

# APPREHENDING MOMENTS

When the siren sounds,
we who have waited at small windows
for moments that stretched to empty years
will shuffle and scrub
the sky's dusty glass
with old skin and knuckles,
hoping to see you forever at last.

Our excitement will overturn small tables
or the fraternal standing-lamp
that has mirrored our stiff vigil of longing
over the lifeless years; and the curtains
that had tied back our wildest wishes
with elegant, waisted forbearance
will crumble to the touch
so that better we can see
and savour the new light,
like a ladle of sweetness at our pumice lips –
and then, O God! that taste of strength
will make us wonder:

How to find the moment
when it is right
to break the womb's estranging glass
and let the withering word
fill our minds and nostrils
with a sharp stagger of pain, like
the punctured lung of loneliness
or love's dangerous balloon
or the *hamartia* of fading yellow roses
waiting for the dry wind to blow.

And if all of this never happens,
how can we look at life?
And how can we ever know?

# APPROACHING LE REPENTIR III
## *Atonement*

It is curious how guilt and pain
bloom and flourish in this land
like the sugar-cane itself... As a
cruel jest of God I was plagued
with success: the price of sugar
soared and my plantations of the
sorrowful names made me rich
enough to afford any physical
comfort or ostentation, and though
I am in hiding from the proprieties
of France, I am prominent here
in Demerara, my word powerful,
my person, amidst the squalid
human debris of two continents,
respected. But peace? Ah peace
is a mountain too high and too far
or simply impossible to find
on this flat and swampy coast...
I am resigned...

If my life seems easy, and my
atonement a trifle too luxurious,
then know that these are just
outward signs: the gilded cover
of the book of me; but on a page
deep within is writ a pain no personal
wealth nor influence can assuage.
I am a man crippled from youth
by an act of horror and I defy
anyone to deny the sincerity of
my penance – enshrined forever

in the names of my plantations.
Even if a great city in the future
were to swallow them up, there
would still (please, God) be a ward,
a suburb, a city square, even
a humble street which will bear
each of the names forever: My only
monuments: *La penitence*, *Le repentir*.

# MOTIVELESS METAPHOR
### (*In memory of Desmond and Alex Abraham*)

Woven into wilderness
was every filament of my desire
those nights when I humbled
to trace and follow the cries
of individual owls,
like startling threads of silver
hunting down the moon.

And something wild in the weft of rivers
summoned through dark undergrowth
to that hem of broken moonlight
leaping from submerged seams of rock
into my fervent eyes
ever scanning the signs for wonders.

Now, not having prepared
for this attenuation of threadbare streets
and infinitely adjustable reading lamps,
I spend the hot, synthetic nights
puzzled in the tombs of books
searching for where it is written
that the greatest love
should fail like rotten fabric
and crumble to expose my dreams – just so.

I string these thoughts like beads
on my single remnant strand of song
so you will know
it is *not* motiveless metaphor

when I rage about the unravelling
of the wilderness of home
and the brilliant death of the chaste moon.
Soon. Death's scissors close too soon.

# APPROACHING LE REPENTIR IV
## *Hetta*

Henrietta Wilhelmina Cendrecourt, my grandmother,
benefited from de Saffon's lifelong guilt:
as a girl who was white, poor, had lost her father
she therefore fit the profile of one entitled
to a share of his penitential legacy: his will directed
that his fortune be used to educate white orphan
(or half-orphan) girls of this purgatorial place…
So it was school till sixteen, then more money
at marriage — she was thus educated and otherwise
endowed when she caught my grandfather's eye.

As a young boy I knew her to be a strong woman
with firm opinions that admitted little argument
and less amendment; quick to discover weakness
and to dismiss the fool, she delighted in her world
of men: six sons, one daughter and the majority
of her grandchildren boys… To ensure that we
would never waste our money on drunken delights,
she dragged us boys to temperance meetings at the Y,
where we sang lustily (with more than half an eye
on the refreshment table): "Alcohol is like a burglar,
never let him in" to the tune of "Coming through the Rye"…

Banished to Georgetown at age nine to attend
a "proper" school, I lived with my grandmother
(my grandfather, those days, seldom strayed
from bed, recovering from a stroke) and got to know her,
finding chinks in her armour, eliciting the occasional
hug — she could be quite tender — and in return
I let myself be paraded at her high teas and
Scrabble evenings… I don't think she knew quite

what to make of me: careless, destructive of tools
and odd bits and pieces that had survived from
my uncles' salad days (I had a talent for exploring
long forgotten shelves and drawers and cupboards)
– and yet I could be quiet, head buried deep in books
(even books that I had no business reading!),
and although at nightfall she'd shoo me to my
homework, she knew she never had to quarrel
about my performance in school: there was
no hint of praise, but I sensed the satisfaction
as she signed the report cards, and that was
enough for me... I learned to be happy.

The time came when both she and I
(with, I would guess, similar reluctance)
followed the rest of our families to Toronto,
fleeing the vulgar coercions of Burnham's land...
We two were the last to stand together
before the maple-leaf flag and call ourselves
Canadian citizens. But Hetta thrived in Toronto,
as she would have done anywhere... even wrote
a memoir (which she entitled "My Derivance"):
I edited and typed it for her and each
of her children got a copy, an egg to hatch into
their own version of family history... She was the
glowing life of her eightieth birthday party; but
it was sad to witness her decline years later,
to glimpse in eyes magnified by thick lenses
that momentary flash of senile panic that
made her wander in quest of somewhere
she called home... And it had to be me
who found her that afternoon, lying dazed
and out of breath, having tripped and fallen beside

a railway track somewhere north of Toronto.
She was following the train line to her house
in Kitty… Later that year she died.

But the Frenchman's lifelong sorrow formed
no part of the legacy Hetta had received.
As I thought about it and listened to her laughter
and her endless stories echoing in my memory,
I came to realize that I was the secret legatee,
the one hounded by guilt and a deeply buried
sadness — not out of regret for any act, but
just for who I am, or who I never allowed
myself to be. And then the fact that I have never
felt entirely free: not from family, not from the
burden of duty, not from God — and yet out of
my secret hurt comes all that defines me:
calm acceptance, success, unexpected, un-
imaginable love — not least for the land of
de Saffon's penitential places… and then…
and then this thing called poetry…

# MIDLIFE: FOUR POEMS

*Nel mezzo del cammin di nostra vita*
*mi ritrovai per una selva oscura*
*ché la diritta via era smarrita*

Dante

1:  *Diagnosis*

Actually, it's hardly a "crisis"
but we like ominous words
that fuel our self-pity and excuse
our impotence – when it comes to the things
we'd rather not get up to.

If I'm honest I will admit that it began
with my body suddenly remembering
the days (and warm, canvas-covered nights)
before it belonged to wife and children
and mortgaged home and hard work
and God –
No, strike God from the list,
for more than ever (and with more joy
than I've known since) it belonged
to that young, handsome, rock-hard God
of river banks and campsites who talked
easy of the body's pleasures,
however derived… who let the
ripple-run of cool creek water
or the belly-skid across wide mud-flats
at low tide whisper about "arousal" and "tumescence"
and the thousands of ritual comings

of age beneath a close, fathering sky
that never thundered its moral imperatives...

You could have predicted the trigger —
some young interloper who reminds you so much
of Adam, or was it Olive or Ann or Hammie —
something in the toss of his/her long hair
and that touch of a hand that shoots
electric memoranda to a long-unopened
file-folder in your overworked brain...
And there is that wicked grin again
and the finger-stroke on tight, trembling belly-skin;
the lowering of long-respected barriers
like impatient undergarments, and then
the naked truth:

that it is impossible to bury forever
the body's oldest longings, especially
when the mind begins to have doubts
about immortality and eternal youth...

## 2: *None So Blind…*

It's frightening how easy it is
to conspire with the world that loves you
in the subversion of all its values.
Somewhere in the long drought of midlife
my body's insistent longing begets
the destroyer whom all mistake
for the victim: "It must have been
some terrorist attack from within," they say,
"born of overwork or anxiety or loneliness —
the mind, you know, is such a fragile thing…"

And it takes the very minimum of guile
to manipulate all the known realities
to mask that central thief,
that naked, grinning, anarchic youth
whose eyes taunt you with their suggestion
that you may be long past enjoying the pleasures
promised in his perfection of look and limb.
These days you only glimpse such delights
in guilty moments, in the rear-view mirror
of your own fading past. Now
here it is incarnate again at last.
God! Surely the more serious sin
is to walk away from this most glorious gift
and to settle for the occasional, well-rehearsed
rubbing (under cover of darkness)
of thankfully forgetful bodies
practising to be corpses.

I want to be able to shout:
"Look at me, I'm alive again
because my love and I built a secret room

where my replenished gift of rain
can end the drought and our love —
all love — can bloom…"
But the faces all turn away
as (the poet once reminded us)
from Breughel's falling Icarus…

But in this case it is neither
the inadvertence of blindness
nor a deliberate refusal to see:
I remove a thirty-year-old beard
and all smile knowingly; they look
into my eyes and see everything.
Everything except me.

3: *Do Not Mistake This For Love*

Do not mistake this for love:
it does not matter
that I close my eyes
and breathe your name when you touch me –
thereabouts...
Cherish your doubts:
they are more faithful
than the plans and wishes
that seem to spring
from these singing nerves that urge us
into ever-new ecstasy...
Do not mistake this for love.

Even when my deepest sigh
lets you know, with certainty,
that your tongue is a welcome guest
in mouth, in navel, across
warm acres of inner thigh...
Do not believe that oldest lie:
do not mistake this for love.

For love seeks to change us
to chain our happy "now"
to an impossible "after",
a place without your laughter.
We have no need of love
nor the heavy door it always opens
into that most chaste purgatory –
some call it "home".
I know, I live there (when I have to)
and it is not the place

for you and me.
Do not mistake the pleasure we make
for love.

So when this moment,
like our frenzied blood, subsides,
and returning reason tries
to talk of love – and consequences –
do not listen, Love,
to those familiar lies.

There is only your flesh and mine,
and the happiness we wring
from just this moment in time.
Beyond this our mortal bodies cannot move:

do not mistake all of this for love.

4: *World without end*

All life's arrangements end:
jobs and homes and families end
and the poet tells us there are tears
for these and for all other things —
"*lachrimae rerum*" — but poets tell us
only what we have always known.

How can I, in this mortal midway,
not know about tears and ashes?
I make my bed between the losses
of the past and tomorrow's damp dawn
of sorrows, the grey light of which I see already:
especially your leaving me,
as your own mind in turn insists
that you discard the tattered book of my flesh
for new pages filled with the wonder,
the crispness the intoxicating musk
of youth and novelty. I know: it was this
I sought and found in you. With this
I am eternally blessed. You should know
that whenever your going comes, it is
already forgiven — and probably for the best.

"World without end" is from a prayer
I have long discarded — yet
as long as you permit me to measure
the joy of my living upon the
still hard and slender frame of your flesh,
there can be no end —
and indeed no world — other than
the network of our nerves
humming in harmony the only song

our bodies know by heart. Why
listen for the notes to fade and die?
Oh my Love, while time permits us yet to see
this mortal day, hour, minute,
let it be filled to the brim
only with you and me.

# MEMORANDUM: THE WORK OF ART IN A34

(This was written in response to a memo sent to all members of staff on
the approach of the University's 50th anniversary. They were trying to
put together a travelling art exhibition and the memo said simply: "If
there are any works of art owned by the University in your office, please
indicate below.")


Thought you'd never ask...
Yes, there's a fine piece in room A34,
it's a mobile nude,
somewhat dated, perhaps,
(produced in the late forties –
by the usual process, in-
volving male and female moulds
and a little lost wax)
draped in old clothing, of course,
so as not to offend the students
or the cleaning lady.

It's been around for years
although not many have noticed;
it's a bit out of shape these days,
but could easily be dusted off
to become part of the travelling exhibit:
colleagues at Mona and St Augustine
might remember it and be pleased
to see it again.

It's about six foot high,
brown, balding and fairly benign,
weighs two hundred pounds –
oh, and of course it belongs to U.W.I.

U.W.I. feeds, clothes, houses
and harasses it,
and threatens it with pension or penury
or both, and generally uses and abuses it
with abandon... In recent times
it's been made to jump through various hoops:
"new semester system", "restructuring",
"committee on governance"... not to mention
the pouring of new foundation
courses on its bewildered head.

Yes, U.W.I. owns it
lock, stock and beard:
were this not the case
it would long have disappeared.
A brief respite for it
would be like heaven...

Collect it any morning, before eleven.

# FOUR POEMS IN DRY SEASON
*(For Juan at the summer solstice)*

— My soul thirsteth for thee, my flesh also longeth after thee:
in a barren and dry land where no water is…

— Psalm 63, *Book of Common Prayer*

## 1: *Dry Season*

When all the tears have been shed
and still the hurt remains, dry,
stuck somewhere in your throat…
then you look at your hands, palms up,
and wonder at your own weakness:
the inability to wrench or shape solutions,
to wring happiness out of situations
that become impossible. And you shrug:
you always knew there were limits
to human endeavour but it aches to discover
that there are limits to hope. And then,
perhaps, you realize what death
is all about. Love, they say, cannot die,
and you like to believe that, but it hurts
to realize that undying love can kill,
so slow and so painfully… Perhaps it were better
if love could — if it did — die, before eyes
and heart and soul become so dry!

## 2: *Life's Dust*

I have begun to gather life's dust;
it's not really visible, yet, but I can
feel it when I touch myself — the texture
of my flesh's longing is somehow altered,
occluded by a granular sensation, the
dry grit of all the years of frustration;
it is not yet enough to chafe and make me sore
but a small discomfort nags each time I
(or some patient, habitual lover) run(s)
a hopeful finger over back or chest or thigh...
I still think it best to ignore such evidence,
to let clear memories of times long before
replace the present patina of regret.
The truth is (and I still believe in truth!)
that my long dry season has caused life's
dust to bloom everywhere; I can still
ignore it on my outer surfaces, but I worry
that deep inside — in belly's churning bowl, in
each lung-pumped puff of breath, or like
a light shroud on my hopeless heart — lies
that same dust of life, covering, contaminating all...
and why do I feel that there is *some*one,
*some*where, who can wash me with a single
tear or breathe sharply on me the gust
that will blow me back to love and wonder —
and life without the dust?

## 3: *Bone Love*

In this season, hot and dry as the dust
that blows in from the public road
— so dry that not even sweat comes to mind —
it seems appropriate to imagine our bones
making love… It is mid-afternoon and
there is no breeze; in fact the sea beyond the wall
may have long since dried up, migrated to
purer climes — anyway, in the background
Dexter Gordon on the sax is playing
*Willow weep for me*, or perhaps Bob is laying
down the rhythm for our love: "coming in,
coming in, coming in, coming in, coming
in from the cold…" and as we get closer,
the clatter of grinding pelvic bones and stick-
fighting femurs threatens to drown the music,
until it all climaxes in a few puffs of seminal dust
that alter absolutely nothing.

Yeah, it's only a dream, but such dreams
are what haunt me these days as I contemplate
my own withering, un-watered, unrequited love,
daring, for the millionth time to hope for even
the shadow of a sigh in response. A poet once said:
"The grave's a fine and private place" and that
sounds about right to me now; perhaps it's time to
haul my weary bones there and wait for you…

## 4: *Dreaming of Rain*

I touch a finger to my dry lips, intending a call
for silence. It is a useless gesture, for no one
speaks any more in this hollow place: all are
afraid of the echoes. But that finger on my
withered lips awakens a skeletal memory of
other lips, touching my own, gesture of something
else, that I seem to have forgotten – except that
it is somehow a signature of you… and I am
anxious again, filled with the old desire that
nothing can assuage nor fulfil, and I remember
the hurt, the heart I had forgotten, the hum
of singing nerves before they turned to dust…
So, since I got this far without intending it,
I may as well take the dream and drive it to its end:

I'll have *this* handsome face, *these* greenish
eyes looking into mine, *these* dry lips, curling
at the corners like the flames that will consume us,
the rasp of *this* shadowed cheek against my own…
There will be abundant kindling: dry grass,  leaves,
faggots, yellow newspaper turning to dust – and
just as the match is struck to end it all in fire,
there is the explosion of thunder and fierce drops
of rain fall and moisten the lips about to kiss…
and I dream of sweet redemption for the world.

# POSTSCRIPT: LOOKING BACK
## (*For Bobby Fernandes*)

After he had signed his will and was ready
for death, did the Frenchman look back
on the one mistake that overtook his life,
that acquainted him with this place, that
filled his mouth with names for sorrow?
And how does one look back? From
the entrance to *Le Repentir* all one sees
is the life of the city: the streets and ways
by which one could have arrived...
How does one recall *exactly* the route taken?

In a grid-patterned city like Georgetown,
all turned corners are optional, all mistaken
ways recoverable (all quarrels reconcilable,
all sins forgivable), and yet, when pushed,
one will still fall – down to the grit of regret,
bruising knee and raw spirit, down the grass
parapet and into the trench of shame,
emerging with the stench of the world's
laughter, clinging wetly like muddy garments...

Or pushed perhaps into forbidden alleyways,
detours and diversions toxic to the spirit,
like sexual deviations that occlude
the steadfast clarity of self-image,
that unravel the great shroud of reputation,
so that one arrives here, in the end, at
*Le Repentir*, in threadbare condition,
hastily wrapped, yet exposed at last
(or as always!) like the cemetery itself,
now so horribly overgrown and neglected –

a sign perhaps of civic grief and the national
disorder that spawns our madness and our
murders in the name of money or drugs or dread –
or (worst of all) the idea of purity –
none of which have any meaning
when committed to the damp earth...

So our places of death, like our lives,
are tainted with the rot, the disorder
of our quest for purities and ascendancies
(that, out of spite, beget their opposites)
racial, moral, religious, individual – De Saffon
understood perhaps all such vain hopes
with their compromises, their regret and their pain...

The criminals that sprout like the weeds
in our burial place are rehearsing only
their own funerals, their disappearance into
this chaotic ground, sans money, sans drugs
sans reputation – which leaves only a name,
like *Le Repentir*, lonely as the ache of eternal
regret, which blooms like a poisonous dust
in the souls of the selfish, the unjust...

Yet we live with the transfiguration of rain
and bright sunlight on wet grass, with
the daily resurrection of skies blue enough
to bring about the consecration of sorrow,
of memory, of hope – and thoughts of that chalice
filled with the blood of love, and the Amen
of forgiven yesterdays, the Amen of all tomorrows.

# ABOUT THE AUTHOR

Professor Mark McWatt was born in Guyana in 1947. He took his first degree at the University of Toronto, then went to Leeds University to complete a Ph.D. He has recently retired as Head of the English Department at the University of the West Indies, Cave Hill campus, Barbados. He has published two collections of poetry, *Interiors* (1989) and The *Language of Eldorado* (1994) that won the Guyana Prize. He has published widely in journals on aspects of Caribbean literature and is joint editor of the *Oxford Book of Caribbean Verse* (2005). His collection of short stories, *Suspended Sentences: Fictions of Atonement*, won the overall best first book Commonwealth Writers Prize in 2006.